How to Find Your Passion

23 Questions That Can
Change Your Entire Life

Michelle Kulp

Table of Contents

Introduction

One question has the power to completely transform your entire life.

Einstein once said, "If I had an hour to solve a problem and my life depended on the solution. I would spend the first 55 minutes determining the proper question to ask; for once I know the proper question, I could solve the problem in less than five minutes."

Einstein was a brilliant man.

In his #1 Wall Street Journal bestselling book, *The One Thing*, Gary Keller, founder of Keller Williams Realty, Inc., wrote:

"Life is a question. You may be asking, 'Why focus on a question when what we really crave is an answer?' It's simple. Answers come from questions, and the quality of any answer is directly determined by the quality of the question. Ask the wrong question, get the wrong answer. Ask the right question, get the right answer. Ask the most powerful question possible, and the answer can be life altering."

Over the years, I too have learned the power of asking the right questions.

This is a story of a powerful question that changed the trajectory of my life...

On October 23, 1992, I serendipitously met country music singer and actor Billy Ray Cyrus after a concert he performed at and had the pleasure of spending a few hours chatting with him. During our time together, Billy Ray asked me:

"What are your dreams?"

At the time, my marriage had recently ended. I was struggling to financially support my three children, living paycheck-to-paycheck in a high-stress job in the legal field, I was having severe panic attacks that led me to the emergency room where I thought I was having a heart attack, and my older brother and best friend, Michael, was diagnosed with AIDS and was dying. I was 29 years old.

Needless to say, it was a dark time in my life and I was living in survival mode. I didn't have the time or energy to think about "dreams."

When you are struggling and in survival mode, you simply don't have the capacity to reflect on higher level things like *dreams*.

Abraham Maslow spoke about this in his hierarchy of needs which are:

- **Basic Needs** – Physiological Needs: food, water, warmth, rest

- **Safety Needs** – security, safety

- **Belongingness and Love Needs** – intimate relationships, friends

- **Esteem Needs** – prestige and feelings of accomplishment

- **Self-Actualization** – achieving one's full potential, including creative activities

Anyone struggling to get their basic physical and/or psychological needs met is not in a frame of mind to focus on self-actualization.

Billy Ray's question struck a chord deep inside of me. During our conversation, Billy Ray said, "We all have a dream buried inside of us and it's our job to go out and find that dream and once we do, we must never ever give up on our dream."

I took Billy Ray's advice and went out searching for this elusive dream; the one that would bring me a deep feeling of purpose, passion and fulfillment; the things that were severely lacking in my life at the time.

It took about a year of soul-searching before I figured it out. Once again, it was because of a question I read in a tiny book that fell into my hands at the bookstore. That book was *How to Find Your Mission in Life* by Richard Bolles.

When I read the question, I immediately knew the answer and what my dream was. I suddenly felt renewed and alive with purpose, passion and direction in my life.

The life-changing question in Richard Bolles book was "What do you love to do where you lose all sense of time?"

Pause and think about that question for a few moments before reading on.

When I read that question and reflected on it, I suddenly drifted back to my childhood remembering how I loved to write; how five hours of writing seemed like five minutes to me. I loved writing poetry, essays, short stories and even reports for school. Writing is where I lost all sense of time.

Unfortunately, as we "grow up" and become adults, we leave behind our childhood interests and passions and take the more practical path of getting a job that pays the bills. We often choose salaries over our soul's aspirations.

The unfortunate part is that when you're stuck in a job you hate, it can feel like a prison.

I worked in the legal field as a paralegal in a high-stress environment for 17 years until I couldn't breathe any longer. It was literally sucking the life out of me.

I wrote about how I freed myself from job prison in my book, *Quit Your Job and Follow Your Dreams: A 12-Month Guide to Being Joyfully Jobless*. Now, I teach others how to do the same.

Rumi reminds us, "What you are seeking is seeking you."

When Billy Ray Cyrus asked me that question about what my dreams were, it started me down a path which eventually led me to the answer I was looking for.

This book contains 23 life-altering questions. Before we begin, my first question for you is:

Do you listen to your head more than your heart?

Too often, we make decisions solely from our logical minds, and that might be okay for a while, but when we are experiencing deep feelings of unhappiness, unfulfillment and purposelessness, it's time for a change and a new direction.

If we make decisions solely from our logical minds, we leave our heart and soul out of the equation. When we do that, we often feel depleted, drained as well as mentally, physically, spiritually and emotionally worn out.

The 23 questions in this book are designed to help you find your passion.

Do not rush through the book. Read each question and the short chapter, then contemplate your answer and write it out in longhand. Search your heart and soul, and not your logical mind.

Before we dive into the questions, I have some tools that I've been using for over 25 years that I believe can help connect your head to your heart during this journey so you can hear the answers deep inside.

Tuning In Tools

I was sitting in my therapist's office when suddenly she announced, "I know your problem Michelle; your heart and head aren't connected."

She was right. I spent my entire life listening to my "head" and completely ignoring my heart.

The decisions I made up to that point were practical and based on obligation and responsibility and left my heart out of the equation.

It's been a long arduous journey connecting my heart and my head, and thankfully I discovered some tools that have helped me along the way. I want to share those tools with you now so you can receive the same benefit as I have using them.

Two of the tools (*The Morning Pages and the Artist Date*) are from Julia Cameron, a recovered blocked artist and author of the bestselling book, *The Artist Way: A Spiritual Path to Higher Creativity.*

I'm adding one more tool of my own which will help quiet down your egoic mind and help tune you into the whispers of your heart and soul: *meditation.*

It's not required that you use these tools, but if you are overly practical, responsible, conscientious and deeply connected to your logical mind like I am, I truly believe it will help you tremendously.

Let's begin...

Morning Pages

In her book, *The Artist Way,* Julia Cameron introduces two pivotal tools in 'creative recovery' which are the *morning pages* and the *artist date.*

In order to retrieve your creativity and your passion, you need to find them. The morning pages are a vehicle that will help you do that.

Morning pages are simply three pages of longhand writing, strictly stream-of-consciousness writing. You might think of them as *brain drain*.

There is no wrong way to do the morning pages. They are a primary tool of creative recovery and finding your passion which is part of that creative recovery.

Unfortunately, we are all victims of our inner critic, inner perfectionist and our inner trouble maker.

This is not the truth of who we are or what we are capable of doing. These collective inner voices are a blocking device that keep you from your creativity and your passions.

By writing three pages in a notebook or journal every morning, you will get to the other side of your inner censor, trouble maker and critic.

It doesn't matter what you write about. Just write without thinking about what you're writing. No one is going to see your morning pages so you can vent, complain, cuss, fuss, nag, protest, process, imagine, dream and invent.

The morning pages will feed your inner artist and you will begin hearing that quiet voice within and eventually you will connect with your own quiet center.

Logic brain is our survival brain and it fears the unknown. Logic brain tells us to be responsible and sensible always.

Artist brain is our creative and holistic brain that wants to come out and play!

Don't underestimate the power of the morning pages as they are a spiritual practice and they will lead you to your inner power and your own source of wisdom.

The only rules are that you write your morning pages as soon as you wake up (stream of consciousness writing) and that you write three pages in longhand in a notebook or journal that you do not share with others. That's it.

Morning pages help chart our own inner interior and without them our dreams and passions will remain buried.

After you are consistent with them, morning pages will point out the need for a *course adjustment*.

Here's what Julia Cameron says about morning pages:

- Your morning pages are your boat. They will both lead you forward and give you a place to recuperate from in your forward motion.

- …writing pages can open an inner door through which our creator helps and guides us. Our willingness swings this inner door open. The morning pages symbolize our willingness to speak to and hear God…it is very powerful.

- The snowflake pattern of your soul is emerging. Each of us is a unique, creative individual. But we often blur that uniqueness with sugar, alcohol, drugs, overwork, underplay bad relations, toxic sex, under-exercise, over-TV, under-sleep—many and varied forms of junk food for the soul. The pages help us to see these smears on our consciousness.

I love what May Sarton, author of dozens of inspirational books including *Journal of a Solitude* says "It always comes back to the same necessity: go deep enough and there is a bedrock of truth, however hard."

ACTION STEP: Purchase a notebook or journal, label it and start your morning pages tomorrow.

The next tool up is the artist date…

Artist Date

On the surface, this may seem like a distraction or a diversion, but the artist date is very powerful and is designed to bring you more insight, inspiration and guidance.

An artist date is just a block of time – two hours per week – where you set aside time to nurture your creative consciousness; your inner artist.

Your artist needs to be taken out, listened to, indulged and pampered. Think of your inner artist like a child and the artist date is self-nurturing to your child artist.

I find when I set aside this time for my artist date that all kinds of emergencies and crises oddly happen that block my artist date from happening.

When we are following our passions and purpose, we have to fight off a force called "the *resistance*" that does not want us to grow, evolve or succeed.

Steven Pressfield, the author of several bestselling books like *The War of Art* and *Turning Pro: Tap Your Inner Power and Create Your Life's Work* explains this resistance we all have to face like this:

"Resistance stops us from committing to the important work of our lives – not just committing to it, but fighting like hell to get it done."

He goes on to explain that *the resistance* hates two qualities above all others: Concentration and Depth. *Why?* Because when we work with focus and we work deep, we succeed.

This *resistance* wants us to stay unfocused and shallow – in other words checking social media 50 times a day, getting caught up in other people's drama, watching endless amounts of television and binging on Netflix instead of doing deep work and activities that are meaningful to our heart and soul that we are *called* to do.

In her book, *Big Magic*, Elizabeth Gilbert, says:

"The universe buries strange jewels deep within us all, and then stands back to see if we can find them.

The hunt to uncover those jewels – that's creative living. The course to go on that hunt in the first place – that's what separates a mundane existence from a more enchanted one."

Just know that when you set aside time for your morning pages and artist dates (your creative work), everything that can block you from using these powerful tools will happen. Don't let it.

Creative living is a path for the brave. It takes courage, persistence, having a daily practice and moving past your fears.

So plan your artist date and watch all kinds of blocks happen. Rise above them.

Keep your artist date sacred and treat it like an appointment with a Very Important Person, and that VIP is your inner artist child! If you have to reschedule, make sure you put it on the calendar or you will completely forget about it.

Artist Dates don't have to be expensive outings. If you are low on cash here are some ideas:

- Go to a local park, lake or beach.

- Go to a pottery place and create art or just observe others.

- Go to a museum.

- Attend an artist event.

- Go to a cooking store and explore.

- Take a hike with beautiful scenery.

- Attend a paint night.

Any activity that makes your inner artist happy!

ACTION STEP: Go ahead and schedule your first two artist dates on your calendar and watch the resistance show up and try to block them. Don't let it!

Next up is the final tool – *meditation*.

Meditation

Michael Singer, author of the bestselling book *The Untethered Soul* says, "When you contemplate the nature of Self, you are meditating, that is why meditation is the highest state. It is the return to the root of your being, the simple awareness of being aware."

Meditation stops the incessant chatter going on in your mind and allows you to connect to your true self. We all have this "monkey mind" that never stops. We wake up in the morning and these thoughts take over our minds like little monkeys jumping from tree to tree. Meditation helps the monkey become still and listen.

Meditation is a very powerful tool. You can start with a few minutes a day and gradually increase the time. I started with two minutes a day and I now do 20 minutes a day.

Spiritual teacher Pema Chodron, says this about meditation:

"Meditation is a process of lightening up, of trusting the basic goodness of what we have and who we are, and of realizing that any wisdom that exists, exists in what we already have. We can lead our life so as to become more awake to who we are and what we're doing rather than

trying to improve or change or get rid of who we are or what we're doing. The key is to wake up, to become more alert, more inquisitive and curious about ourselves."

– Pema Chodron

Meditation has changed my life, taken away my anxiety and helped me to connect to my heart and soul.

Meditation is a tool I recommend as you do this deep work.

ACTION STEP: Download a meditation app and start with 2-5 minutes of meditation today. I use the app called "Chime".

Now it's time to get started on the 23 questions that can change your entire life…

Chapter 1: Hate

Question: What do I absolutely hate about or hate doing in my job or in my life? (Be specific)

Sometimes when we're lost and confused, we don't know what we're looking for or what exactly it is that we want.

I've found we can get clues by starting with what we *hate* or what isn't working.

These clues can lead you to what you do want.

For example, let's say you have a job as a paralegal (as I once did) and you are spending 80% of your time at the computer. You hate spending time at the computer, so you write "I hate sitting at a computer for 8 hours a day."

This insight gives you the ability to change things in your life that are draining you and also prevents you from repeating them down the road. I know a lot of people who change jobs without taking the time to figure out why they hated their jobs, only to end up repeating the pattern and hating the next job.

You can also write about things you hate in your personal life.

- I hate going to the grocery store.

- I hate cleaning the house.

- I hate volunteering on specific committees.

Don't be afraid to be radically honest with yourself. You can't get to the truth if you aren't being honest; the words you are writing are for your eyes only.

For example, when I was raising three kids as a single mom, it was highly stressful. I was a working mom and I looked forward to going to my job at the law firm. I respect stay-at-home moms, but there is no way I could have been one full-time. I think it would have driven me mad. I loved my career for many years when I was in it and it also supported my family.

So be completely honest about what you *hate* in your life right now. It doesn't mean you have to quit your job or divorce your spouse or live like a slob or eat out at restaurants all the time.

We're looking for clues here that will lead to your passion. Think of these questions as a means to an end. The questions will help you get more clarity in your life.

Hate is a strong emotion so pay attention to it.

When I started my online business www.becomea6figure-woman.com in 2005, I had a fairly large house and I "hated" cleaning it. I remember saying to my best friend that I would rather figure out how to make more money and pay for a cleaning company than to clean it myself. And that's exactly what I did.

I got creative and started selling online courses from my website and then I was able to pay for a cleaning company to take care of the house.

What do you *hate* in your life right now?

Notes

Chapter 2: Youth

*Question: When I was a youngster,
I always wanted to...?*

What kind of things did you like as a child?

Did you love being outdoors?

Were you a bookworm?

Did you love writing? Drawing?

Did you love pretending to be a firefighter or a police officer?

Did you play dress up?

Did you love make up?

Did you love cooking?

Did you love swimming, hiking or fishing?

What kind of kid were you?

Your childhood often holds clues to your passions. When I started reflecting back to my childhood, I remembered how much I loved writing. I also loved being outdoors, riding my bike, putting on neighborhood skits, going to the beach and I loved reading books.

This is the time to remember things you loved about your childhood and that you found a lot of happiness and joy doing.

Again, these are little clues we are looking for to help us remember.

The reason you're reading this book is because you're having a bit of amnesia about your passions and you're probably making most of your choices based on safety and security instead of your imagination, joy and fun!

So play a little and go back to your youth and see what you can remember.

As a child, I loved putting on neighborhood skits and entertaining people. I involved my three brothers and my best friend who lived next door and we had so much fun. We actually made money selling tickets to our events.

As a teenager and adult, however, I was very shy and self-conscious. Eventually, I realized my shyness was holding me back in life. I wanted to be that fun, outgoing person again like I was when I was a child.

So, I enrolled in Toastmasters and was a member for many years. I even became President of my local club and eventually I was Area Governor.

Then, I found *Speaking Circles®* which was about learning to speak from the heart and connect with people through relational presence.

Speaking Circles changed my life and I eventually became a facilitator helping others who were struggling with speaking and connecting.

Without Speaking Circles, I would probably still be a very shy introvert. Now, I happily do speaking engagements, teach workshops and I love working with people.

Go back to your childhood and remember what you loved doing and what came so natural to you.

Notes

Chapter 3: Guidance

*Question: What do people come
to me for advice or guidance about?*

People always come to me for:

- Legal advice because I was a paralegal for 17 years (even though I've been out of the legal field for almost 20 years now).

- Advice about writing and/or publishing books since I have my online business www.bestsellingauthorprogram.com

- Details on how to start an online business, make six figures and find their passion.

I am asked for guidance on these topics because I have done all those things myself.

So what do people come to you for advice? Not just in business, but on a personal level too?

I am also often asked for cooking and decorating advice because I love cooking and decorating, they come natural to me and I truly enjoy them.

Think about what questions people ask you about when they need help or guidance. This can be a clue to what others see you as skilled at and that you might just take for granted.

I used to think everyone was a great writer until I taught business writing at the community college and quickly realized a lot of people struggle with writing and don't like it.

The reason we take our gifts for granted is because when something comes natural to us, we don't see it as something special, but instead we see it as an ordinary part of who we are.

Write down at least three things
people come to you for advice on.

Notes

_____

_____

_____

_____

_____

_____

_____

_____

_____

_____

_____

_____

_____

_____

_____

_____

_____

_____

Chapter 4: Time

***Question: What do I love to do where
I lose all sense of time while doing it?***

I'm very fond of this question because it changed my whole life. I found the question in Richard Bolle's extraordinary book *How to Find Your Mission In Life* and as soon as I read it I knew the answer: Writing!

I loved to write as a child, as an adolescent and as an adult. The only difference was that the writing I did as an adult was legal writing in my job as a paralegal, but I still *loved* that part of the job.

Writing came natural to me and I never thought about it at all until I read this question; I remembered when I was younger that feeling like time was flying by when I was involved in this activity.

When does time stand still for you when you're involved in something you love? This could be a huge clue to what your passion is.

We can have more than one passion too. I love research almost as much as I love writing. I love teaching as well. There is no rule that you can only have one passion.

I think it's miraculous when you can turn your passions into a profitable business because then you can get paid to play and earn "Play-checks" instead of "Pay-checks."

When you get paid to do what you love, then it doesn't seem like work.

In my online business, I do a lot of writing, research and teaching so I am very happy getting paid to do what I love.

You might have to go back to your childhood and try to remember that feeling when time flew by.

Answer the question from your childhood years and also as an adult.

Is there anything you do in your current life where time flies by?

I love watching the HGTV shows; especially the ones where people relocate to new homes and new states or countries. Often these people had successful corporate careers, but that joy, purpose and fulfillment was missing. So, they took a leap and changed everything including what they did for a living.

I've noticed that most of the time people who were leaving corporate careers were choosing brand new creative careers or starting their own business in a creative field.

What do you love to do where you lose all sense of time? Maybe it's something as simple as baking cupcakes.

Notes

Chapter 5: Guess

If I had to guess what my passion is, I would say it is...?

When Billy Ray Cyrus asked me what my dreams were, my answer at the time was "I don't have any dreams. My life is about survival."

Sometimes, we simply have amnesia when it comes to our dreams and passions.

In my book, *Quit Your Job and Follow Your Dreams*, I talk about the four distinctions of a job, a career, your calling and hobbies that I read in a blog post by Elizabeth Gilbert. These distinctions are detailed below:

Job – You undeniably need a job to pay your bills and you don't have to be in love with your job. It is a means to an end. Money is how we all survive in this world and a job pays the bills. If you despise your job, by all means get a new one, but a job is vital. Just don't make it your whole life.

Career – A career is different from a job and is something you build over time with passion, energy and commitment. Careers are huge investments and require strategy, hustle and ambition. Not everyone has a career or will have a career and that's okay. A career is a choice.

Calling (vocation) – Vocation comes from the Latin verb "vocare" which means "to call." Your vocation is literally *your calling*. It is an invitation from the Universe and it shows up as your soul calling to you. You do not need to make money from your calling although some people do.

Hobby – Something you do in your spare time for pleasure, relaxation, distraction or curiosity. Hobbies change and your attitude towards them is relaxed and playful. Hobbies are a wonderful reminder that we are not just slaves to the capitalist machine or our own ambitions. You don't need a hobby, but it's sure nice to have one. You do not need to make money from your hobby although some people do.

I hope reading these four distinctions helps you think about your passions in a different context. I see people mixing these up all the time. Making hobbies into jobbies or quitting jobs they aren't in love with but that pays the bills or feeling bad because they don't have a career.

We are all unique and therefore these four distinctions are unique to each of us.

As you reflect on what you think your passions are, think about what brings your soul to life.

Your passions are hinted at through your talents, tastes, excitement and curiosities.

Notes

Chapter 6: Truth

What do I truly want, but don't believe I can ever have?

Is there something you really, really want to have in your life but don't believe you can have it.

I truly want a house on the water. Right now I don't have a house on the water, but I do have a beautiful house across the street from the water with lovely water views. In fact, I can see the water from my bedroom window while sitting at my desk as I am writing this chapter.

The reason I don't have my house on the water is because the price difference between these two houses is substantial. Sometimes I wonder if I will ever have my dream house on the water.

Is there something you truly desire in your life – a relationship, a material possession, a job, starting your own business or maybe it's something emotional --- like less anxiety and more peace.

Write down whatever comes to your mind. No one is judging you. These answers are for your eyes only.

Be honest with yourself about what you want.

For example, I know a lot of independent women who don't want to admit they would love to be in an intimate and committed relationship with a man, but seem conflicted because of their freedom and independence; they feel like they might have to give up some of that freedom to be in a relationship.

Maybe you want more free time in your life to daydream, travel or write. Whatever it is, you're entitled to want those things.

You must be radically honest about your desires if you ever want to achieve them.

I've found another block to wanting things is we don't want to surpass where our family and friends are. We feel bad about doing better than people close to us.

It's time to turn that misguided thinking around and view being successful (however we define it) as a way to help our families and friends. We can also be a role model and an inspiration to others too.

Yes, some people might be jealous, but jealousy usually stems from envy. These people actually envy what you have because they want it for themselves so it comes out negatively as being jealous.

Don't take it personally and don't let it stop you from going after what you truly want in life.

Notes

Chapter 7: Freedom

What gives me a sense of freedom when I do it?

Freedom is everything to me. When I was trapped in my corporate job what I craved most was freedom – time and money freedom.

I wanted control of my time, especially since I was a single mom with three young children. It was awful having to miss out on special events and activities with them as well as struggling with the choice of staying home with a sick child or going to work so I didn't get fired.

I think deep down we all have a desire for freedom; however, many of us fall into the trap of trading in our time for material things and then get stuck in that high-priced lifestyle with a lot of debt.

When I left my corporate job, I made the decision that I would never trade in my freedom for money again. I'm happy to say I've been out of the corporate world for almost 20 years now and *freedom* is the driving factor in my life.

I don't have 100% freedom because I run an online business and I have responsibilities and accountability in my business, but I am free to choose what I do in my business, what hours I work, who I work with and how much money I make…and that is priceless!

So when do you feel freedom in your life? Is it when you are involved in a certain activity or maybe when you are on vacation or when you're not glued to technology?

Take some time to reflect on what *freedom* means to you and look back and see at what times in your life you've felt free.

Looking back at my life, I've had two types of jobs:

1. Energy-draining jobs
2. Freedom jobs

An energy-draining job is one that consumes your time and energy so that at the end of the day you have none left to pursue your passions and curiosities.

If you are going to have a job that pays the bills and gives you freedom to pursue your passions, you want a freedom job.

Going from an energy draining job to a freedom job is a step in the right direction as long as you can figure out the financial part.

I went from a full-time paralegal job to a part-time job at the law firm (working three nights a week from 5:30 p.m. to 12:30 a.m.) and that gave me the *freedom* to pursue my passions. I did that for five years. Then, I found another freedom job which was an outside sales job working 20-25 hours a week and making six figures!

Every step you take in your life should be towards more freedom, not less.

Notes

_____

_____

_____

_____

_____

_____

_____

_____

_____

_____

_____

_____

_____

_____

Chapter 8: Failure

If I knew I couldn't fail, I would be doing ...?

Failure is how we learn. If we're afraid to fail, then we're afraid to learn.

If you knew you couldn't fail, what would you be doing?

Be completely honest with yourself.

We can't let this fear of failure prevent us from following our passions and dreams. We have to do it in spite of those fears.

Every successful person has these fears, they just don't allow these fears to prevent them from achieving their dreams and goals.

You make a choice every single day when you decide *not* to take action towards your goals and dreams.

I can't tell you how many years I struggled with the imposter syndrome around starting and running an online business because I didn't have any "credentials." I finally got over it, but I wasted a lot of time looking for approval, validation and praise instead of just doing what I loved and learning from my failures.

That's what we are all doing. There are no exceptions. Don't let the filtered world of social media taint your view of successful people. They all have fears and are dealing with them in their own way so they can achieve their goals and dreams.

If you have an intense fear of failure, you will waste a lot of time and money looking for external validation and approval instead of doing *the work*.

Years ago, I read a great book by Susan Jeffers called *Feel the Fear and Do it Anyways*. I think the older I get, the less I care about these fears of failure. I know failure is inevitable and it teaches us what works and what doesn't.

Many people want to start an online business, but until you actually put yourself out there and try, you have no idea about the process. It's like writing a book, you can have a great idea and test titles and covers, but until you actually write it and put it out in the marketplace, you won't know if people want it or not.

I tell my clients in my bestselling author program, that we will put out a high quality book with a strong foundation, but at the end of the day, the market decides what it likes.

And guess what?

The market is fickle and constantly changing. So, if you are going to write a book, start a business, I suggest you do it fast.

Another great book I recommend is the *7-Day Start Up: You Don't Learn Until You Launch* by Dan Norris. It will change your entire perspective from inaction to fast action.

So, if you knew you couldn't fail, what would you be doing?

Notes

Chapter 9: Success

***If it was guaranteed I would be
massively successful, I would be ...?***

First, what does massive success look like to you?

One person might say, "Massive success would mean my house is paid off, I have no debt and I can live fully on my retirement money."

Another person might say, "I am living in my mansion on the water with my beautiful boat and three jet skis. I also have lots of passive income from my books and courses that pay all of my living expenses."

Write down what massive success looks like to you because if it is guaranteed then you can dream bigger than you ever have before. Sometimes our fear of not achieving our dreams makes us shrink them or not be real with ourselves about what we truly desire.

I have always wanted a house on the water. I currently live across the street from the water so I am getting closer. It's not my whole dream, but it is a part of my dream. As a writer, the water brings out my creativity and I feel very peaceful being near the water.

Years ago, I saw an interview on a morning talk show with William Haley, the son of Alex Haley, the famous writer and creator of the blockbuster book and miniseries, *Roots*.

Alex Haley's book, *Roots*, sold over one million copies in the first year, and the miniseries was watched by an astonishing 130 million people. It also won both the Pulitzer Prize and the National Book Award.

William was explaining to the reporter that his father said he did his best writing when he was near the water. He would often hop on board a freight or cargo ship and take long trips to do his writing.

Alex Haley said, "I find that's why I just love to get out in the ocean. And I find that you are really out there, find yourself thinking in ways you haven't thought before."

Seeing that interview made me realize how important being near the water is to me; it is magical, miraculous, mysterious and brings out a level of creativity that I just can't find sitting at my computer under artificial lights. I find that being near the ocean also helps me discover answers to my deepest questions.

So, dream big and write down all the details to what massive success looks like to you when you know it's guaranteed!

Notes

Chapter 10: Future

What would the 'future me' - 10 years from now - tell the 'current me' to do?

First, think about what the 'current you' would tell the 'past you' 10 years ago. You've learned a lot in the past 10 years. What words of wisdom can you share with her or him?

I would tell the past me:

- You don't need external approval from others, just follow your heart and trust your intuition.

- Stop trying to do everything in your business by yourself; hire contractors who specialize in what you need for your business and let go of the reins.

- Don't be afraid to hire a business coach as it can change your entire business and will grow your profits exponentially.

- Have a morning routine to start the day off in a conscious, peaceful and intentional way.

- Learn to say 'no' and set boundaries and you will have less drama and miscommunications in your life.

- Create more passive income.

Think about all the areas of your life. Where are you struggling? What do you want your life to look like in ten years?

One goal I have is to generate six figures in "passive" income from the royalties of my books. In order to do that, I'm going to have to make some changes to my schedule, not take on as many done-for-you clients and save more money.

There is research that says a written down goal is 33% more likely to be completed. There is power in the written word.

We think thousands of thoughts every day, but when we consciously and intentionally choose to focus on a few, then our lives change.

Think about the past you 10 years ago, the current you, and now the future you 10 years from now.

What age will you be? Where do you want to be living? What daily activities do you want to be involved in? Who do you want to be spending time with? How do you want to earn money?

Of course, we want some spontaneity in our lives, but we also want to set intentions or else we end up living a default life and before you know it – your life has flown by.

They say the days are long but the years pass by fast.

Notes

Chapter 11: Anger

What makes me so angry and
heated I get all charged up?

There is wisdom in our anger. It's here to tell us something about ourselves. It contains hidden messages.

If we're angry at bouncing a check, then the anger is there to tell you that maybe living paycheck-to-paycheck isn't working and something needs to change.

If we're angry at a client who is being disrespectful or taking advantage of us, then maybe the message is you need to have clearer boundaries or have a signed contract with clients to set the expectations.

If we're angry about domestic violence, maybe we need to get involved in being part of the solution and become an advocate or volunteer.

Usually when I get angry, I've let things go far too long and they've started to fester until finally I have to release some of that steam I've been repressing.

Harriet Lerner, author of *The Dance of Anger*, says, "Anger is a signal and one worth listening to."

Anger has a hidden message for you. Listen to it.

What are you angry about? Be honest? Even if it's something you can't change right now, write it down.

David R. Hawkins, M.D., Ph.D., in his book *Power vs Force*, says that anger stems from "frustrated want."

He also says that "Anger can lead to either constructive or destructive action."

So, anger can lead to constructive action, but if you let it, anger can also lead to belligerence, arguments, irritability, explosiveness, and even rage.

Listen to your anger and see what changes you need to make because of it.

When I was angry at having to go to my 9-5 job at the law firm and leave my kids, my anger was telling me there was another path for me.

Anger can be your friend if you listen to it.

Notes

Chapter 12: Contribution

What would I like to change or contribute in the world?

We all have the ability to contribute something to the world to make it better.

It doesn't have to be large scale or grand, just some way you want to contribute your time, energy, knowledge and expertise to improving the world.

For me, writing books is the way I contribute to the world. The most powerful shifts have happened in my life as a result of books so I know the power of a great book; one sentence in a book can change someone's life.

In the book, *Who Do We Choose to Be: Facing Reality, Claiming Leadership, Restoring Sanity* written by Margaret J. Wheatley, she asks the question:

"If it's not creating change at the large scale…then what does it mean to make a difference?

Her answer…

"Focus on serving others. Serve individuals, serve small groups; serve an entire community or organization. No matter what is going on around us, we can attend to the people in front of us, to the issues confronting us and there, we offer what we can. We can offer insight and compassion. We can be present. We can stay focused and not flee. We can be exemplars of the best human qualities. That is a life well lived, even if we didn't save the world."

Humans cannot live without meaning.

Making a contribution by being of service gives us meaning and purpose.

Think about the people in your life who have been there for you as ground and support; we all stand on the shoulders of others.

At some point, we must be those shoulders for others and that's where service and contribution come in.

Notes

_____

_____

_____

_____

_____

_____

_____

_____

_____

_____

_____

_____

_____

_____

_____

_____

_____

_____

Chapter 13: Practice

If I had time to practice more, I'd be really good at?

In my senior year of high school (circa 1981), I took a typing class. At first, I hated typing and didn't really see the value of learning this skill, but I'm glad I stuck with it.

We had to memorize the location of the keys and be able to type with a piece of copy paper taped above our hands that blocked us from seeing the keys.

It took a lot of practice and I went from pecking at the keys to memorizing all the keys to then typing about 40 words per minute when I graduated from that class.

After graduation, I typed papers when I was in college and then I typed a lot when I worked as a paralegal and legal secretary for many years. The more I used this skill, the better and faster I got. At one point, I was typing 100 wpm.

What could you excel at if you practiced?

People think great writers or great artists are just born; what they don't see are the copious amount of hours of *practice* they spend developing their skills.

Many famous writers are really bad writers at first. They become great writers because they continued to write and they gradually got better. That's the art of practice.

I remember reading a story about a writer who was working on a manuscript for over a year. The writer got to page 200 and realized that was where the story began; so those first 200 pages ended up in the trash.

Can you imagine throwing away 200 pages of a manuscript? As a writer, I know how painful that would be, but those 200 pages essentially were his *practice*.

Practice requires focus and attention.

In Cal Newport's book, *Deep Work: Rules for Focused Success in a Distracted World*, he says:

"To learn hard things quickly, you must focus intensely without distraction. To learn, in other words, is an act of deep work."

We live in a high-distraction world and the ability to focus intensely is getting harder and harder with so many demands on our time.

Imagine for a moment that you can take a break from all distractions – television, social media, text messages, your phone, your job – and you could *practice* one thing…what would that be?

There is no wrong or right answer.

Notes

Chapter 14: Flow

When I am in a state of flow, I am...?

Mihaly Csikszenthihalyi, a well-known psychologist, once said:

"The best moments usually occur when a person's body or mind is stretched to its limits in a voluntary effort to accomplish something difficult and worthwhile."

Csikszenthihalyi calls this mental state *flow* (which was also a book he wrote in 1990 by the same title).

Sometimes we think of *flow* as complete relaxation as in sitting in a hammock, but Csikszenthihalyi's research revealed that human beings are at their best when they are *immersed deeply in something challenging.*

So, think about a time when you were immersed deeply in something challenging and felt you were in that *flow* state.

What were you doing?

For me, the *flow* state happens when I am working on a book. It is challenging and it is something I care deeply about. I also lose my sense of time when I'm doing it.

Bono once said, "Good things come to those who work their asses off and never give up."

I believe that's true. We aren't born to sit around sipping daiquiris at the beach all day. Although having downtime is very important to a creative life, our minds require and also thrive on deep challenging work.

Flow is about stretching your mind to its limits, concentrating and losing yourself in an activity.

Can you think about a time when you felt all three of those? What were you doing? How long were you doing it? What were the results?

Notes

Chapter 15: Interests

I have a lot of interests and things I enjoy,
but if I had to pick only one of those things to spend
time on now, I would choose...?

In his #1 Wall Street Journal bestselling book, *The One Thing*, Gary Keller, founder of Keller Williams Realty, Inc., wrote:

"Going small is ignoring all the things you *could* do and doing what you *should* do. It's recognizing that not all things matter equally and finding the things that matter most. It's a tighter way to connect what you do, with what you want. It's realizing that extraordinary results are directly determined by how narrow you make your focus."

We have no shortage of options of how we can spend our valuable time. In fact, having too many options can lead to decision fatigue or making no decision at all because you're feeling overwhelmed with too many choices.

So, how do we decide on *one thing* when we have so many options to choose from?

Instead of asking yourself, "What do I have to give up?" instead ask yourself, "What do I want to go big on?"

This small change in your thinking can have a profound affect in your life.

Another way to make decisions is to explore and evaluate a **broad set of options** *before* committing to any. This way, you are giving yourself time to play, think, question, listen, try out and debate, and the pressure is minimized. Once you've given yourself the gift of exploring, then you can decide what you want to "go big on."

Think about some of the interests you have right now or in the past that you've explored. If you could only pick one "for right now" (not forever), which one would you go big on?

One of the core premises in *The One Thing* is: **I can do anything, but not everything**.

As poet Mary Oliver wrote, "Tell me what it is you plan to do with your one wild and precious life?"

Notes

_____

_____

_____

_____

_____

_____

_____

_____

_____

_____

_____

_____

_____

_____

_____

_____

Chapter 16: Fears

*My biggest fear about being successful
and living a passionate life is...?*

Years ago, I attended a 3-day event with author T. Harv Eker who wrote the bestselling book *Secrets of the Millionaire Mind.*

During that workshop, we did an exercise to see what fears were stopping us from living our dream life and it turned out my biggest fear was not a fear of failure, but a fear of success.

Sounds crazy, right?

Why would I be afraid of success?

Fears aren't always logical and stem mostly from our emotions.

Since I was a big people pleaser, I thought people wouldn't like me if I was super successful and made more money than they did.

Of course, I turned my thinking around and now I look at all the ways I can inspire others to live their dreams, and also how I am in a position to help my family and friends because

I have financial freedom. I am no longer living paycheck-to-paycheck (which was how I was living at the time of the workshop).

So, what is your biggest fear about being successful and living a passionate life?

When I started www.becomea6figurewoman.com in 2005, I had just started making six figures in 2004. I went from working in a 9-5 corporate job in the legal field to selling hot tubs in-house. I literally doubled my income and my time off! Life was good.

When I was doing research for my website, I noticed that a lot of women said they only wanted to make "enough to pay the bills" and they didn't want to make six figures because they didn't want to work 60+ hours a week and give up time with their family and friends. They assumed you could only make six figures if you worked long hours…which isn't true as I am living proof of that. I still only work about four hours a day, four days a week and make six figures.

It's all about designing a life you want. However, we also have subconscious fears that are blocking us and causing us to sabotage ourselves in the process of going after our dreams.

Pia Mellody, the author of many books on co-dependency once said, "If you don't face your fears, they will bite you in the ass!"

It's true. Your fears will block your success so you need to identify them and face them head on and then take action anyway.

Most fears aren't real and just knowing what they are puts you in a position of power.

So, be radically honest and list your fears out. Then feel the fear and do it anyway!

Notes

Chapter 17: Less

What do you want to have less of in your life?

Cheryl Richardson, Life Coach and Author of *Stand Up For Your Life*, said, "A high quality life has more to do with what you *remove* from it than what you *add* to it."

That sentence has always stuck with me.

Many of us get caught up in the hamster wheel of chasing more, more, more. But there's a price to pay for having more, more, more.

Years ago, I owned a million-dollar house with a million-dollar mortgage. Of course, I had a nice 6-figure income to pay for it all and a fiancé that paid for half at the time, but when the housing market crashed, the value of my million dollar house went to almost half.

My sales income at the time (2008) also decreased as the product I was selling was a luxury product (hot tubs) that people really didn't need.

So, in an instant, my life changed and I had to make some big changes as a result. I sold the million-dollar house and downsized to a smaller home. I am so much happier now because the less I have to pay, the more I can play!

So, what do you want less of in your life? Be specific.

If you say you want less stress, that's very general. Be more specific like, "I want less stress at my job" or "I want less stress in my relationship with _____."

Often, what we want less of can give us clues to changes we need to make in our lives.

Maybe you are always saying yes to others and consequently are overbooked in your schedule. Therefore, you need fewer time commitments and the action you need to take is learning to say no.

In this moment, if I was answering this question, I would say I would want less back and neck issues. I also know that when I consistently do my 20-minute back care yoga DVD and my 3-mile walks, that I reduce my back and neck issues. So, that is a clue letting me know I need to be more consistent with my routine and also less sitting at the computer.

I did purchase a standup desk a couple of years ago so that has helped as well.

This is a great question to ask yourself regularly because sometimes we are just living our lives on autopilot.

Keep removing things you don't want and you'll have a high-quality life.

Notes

Chapter 18: Millions

If I had $10 million dollars in the bank, I would...?

This is a great question. At first you might think, "I'd quit my job, travel to a tropical island and sip margaritas on the beach and chill all day."

Sounds great but I can promise that within a short time you would be bored with that.

As I mentioned in the chapter about *flow*, our minds were created to be stretched and challenged.

I'm not saying you wouldn't quit your job, but you would want to be involved in something you truly care about; even if you didn't get paid for it.

This is an exercise in using your imagination. Money can and does change everything.

Because of my online business, I am able to save a percentage of what I make each year (which happens to be the equivalent of my entire annual salary when I worked as a paralegal in the corporate world). Having this money in the bank gives me more freedom and options. It also helped me with one of my goals – which was to write more books and take on less done-for-you clients for my bestselling author program.

The money I save isn't close to $10 million dollars, but having six figures in the bank gives me a lot more options about my business, my life and where I choose to spend my time.

Besides buying material things like a house, a new car, new furniture and taking some trips, once that was all out of the way, what would you do with your time?

This is a clue to your passions. There are some things we do in life for a paycheck and others are just solely for pleasure or fulfillment. For example, let's say you would like to get involved in a non-profit organization and volunteer. That is something you might be able to do right now that would bring you a great deal of fulfillment and satisfaction in your life.

We're here to be of service to others. Of course, when we're living in survival mode, it's hard to do that, but once we are able to get our finances working for us, then we can look at how we can be of service to others.

After I left the legal field, I wanted to get involved in helping women who were struggling with domestic violence issues and I was able to volunteer for a non-profit organization called the House of Ruth that provided legal services for people dealing with domestic violence. This gave me a high level of fulfillment because I was using my legal knowledge to help others.

Maybe you want to start your own business. So many people have that dream, but the obstacles are usually lack of time and/or money.

Dream big.

What type of business would you want to start? Give details about what you would do with $10 million.

Notes

_____

_____

_____

_____

_____

_____

_____

_____

_____

_____

_____

_____

_____

_____

_____

_____

_____

Chapter 19: Others

*If I didn't care what other people thought or
how it might affect them, I would be …?*

Is there something you are not doing because of what others might think? Or maybe you're doing a lot of things out of obligation and therefore if you stop doing them, they would impact others negatively.

I have a high level of the "disease to please" and I tend to do for others what they can do for themselves. I've done it with my children and in relationships, but at the end of the day, it leaves me exhausted, resentful and unhappy. My "overdoing" means I'm putting other people's happiness and needs above my own.

Some people say you need to be more selfish. I even saw a woman on a talk show wearing a necklace that read "Selfish."

It's not so much about being "selfish," but it is about caring enough about your "self" to put your needs, desires, energy, time, money, and dreams at the top of the list.

A book I read that helped me do this was *Boundaries: When to say Yes, How to Say No to Take Control of Your Life* by Dr. Henry Cloud and Dr. John Townsend. In that book the authors said:

"People with boundary problems usually have distorted attitudes about responsibility. They feel that to hold people responsible for their feelings, choices and behaviors is mean."

I know I felt that way. I didn't want to let people down and I wanted to help, but my actions resulted in enabling others.

They also say that a boundary shows you where you end and someone else begins.

So, do you have clear boundaries with others?

If not, you may not be taking the path to your dreams because of distorted responsibilities and the disease to please.

It's hard to imagine not caring about what others think, but the older I get the less I seem to care. I do what makes me happy as long as it does no harm to others.

Imagine doing what you truly want to do and not wondering what others think or how it might affect them.

What would you be doing right now?

Notes

Chapter 20: Obstacles

What are three ways you create obstacles in your life and why?

There is an ancient saying: "The road is smooth. Why do you throw rocks before you?"

I'm sure you can relate to this as I know I can.

Why do we throw rocks on the road before us?

Self-sabotage is a real thing that we do when we are afraid or don't feel deserving of something or are stuck and unable to take action.

We all have sabotaged ourselves so don't feel bad about it. Observation without condemnation is a great viewpoint to follow.

Think about three ways you have created obstacles in your life and then write down why you think you have done that.

For many years, I lived paycheck-to-paycheck and I blamed everyone else for my money problems. Then one day, I heard one of my mentors say, "Take 100% responsibility for everything in your life." And when I did take 100% responsibility, I realized I had the power to change my financial situation.

Now I save 25-50% of my income every year and don't live on the financial edge any longer.

Life Coach, Author, Speaker and Talk Show host, Mel Robbins, said, "If you have a problem that can be fixed by action, then you really don't have a problem."

Sometimes we create problems by our inaction and procrastination. Think about a time perhaps when a bill came due and you procrastinated about paying it and then you had terrible consequences. If you would have just paid it when you received it (taken action), you wouldn't have had those consequences.

Living a life of passion requires action. You can't get other people to do your push-ups for you. Only you can do them. We can try to blame our parents, our spouse, our children, our family, our geography, or our life situation, but at the end of the day, we have the power to take action and make changes.

Start noticing when you are procrastinating and journal about why you aren't taking action. Usually, it's an emotional block and you can journal through it.

The problem is most of the time, we don't bring it to our awareness and our unconscious minds are running the show.

What are these areas of your life and the three ways you have created obstacles? Are they all in finance, relationships, business, etc.? Take notice and examine the feelings underneath your inaction.

Notes

Chapter 21: Principle

What principle, cause, value or purpose would you be willing to defend to the death or devote your life to?

Billy Sunday once said, "More men fail through lack of purpose than through lack of talent."

I have a few things that motivate me:

1. Family

2. Freedom

3. Finances

When I was stuck in my 9-5 corporate job, I had no freedom and now that I'm out of that life, I value my freedom more than anything.

My family means everything to me and so that motivates me to be successful and to be a great example.

Having my finances in order gives me *freedom* and options. As I mentioned earlier, I'm now able to save 25-50% of my income every year. There was a time when I was making six figures and had very little in my savings account. My goal now is to save 50% of my income and this year I'm focusing more on leveraging my time and creating additional passive income streams.

What motivates you? It could be a value like freedom or justice; or a cause like helping feed the homeless; or a purpose like changing lives through speaking or writing.

Books are part of my life purpose and are very important to me personally because books have changed my life and saved my life in many ways. I know the power of a book and that's why I'm so passionate about them. It is part of my purpose to spread powerful messages to the world with my own books and with my clients books.

Think about things that have changed your life or saved your life. Have you ever heard the saying "Make your mess your message." What messes have you been in? What obstacles have you overcome?

Many times, our purpose involves helping other people overcome those same messes we've been in.

Notes

Chapter 22: Inner Voice

*What has your inner voice been saying
to you that you have been ignoring?*

One of my favorite authors is Richard Bode who wrote, *First You Have to Row a Little Boat* and *Beachcombing at Miramar.* In his book, he said, "I believe we are born with a power to heal our wounds, not through miracles, but through a silent voice that speaks to us from within ourselves and won't be stilled; a voice that tells us where to go and what to do, which is a miracle of another kind. It is the refusal to heed that inner voice that causes the incurable sickness of the soul which makes us wither before our time."

Are you ignoring your inner voice? Ghosting it?

After I left the legal field, I started practicing meditation every morning. Soon, my inner voice repeatedly said, "It's time to get over your fear of public speaking. If you don't get over it, it will hold you back from becoming a successful writer."

Now this made no sense to my logical mind so I ignored it for a long time. But the voice was relentless. It wouldn't go away.

My logical mind kept trying to figure out what in the world public speaking had to do with writing?

Eventually, I surrendered and listened to my inner voice. I joined Toastmasters and within a short time and against all odds, I became President and Area Governor. That led me to Speaking Circles® which I spoke about in an earlier chapter and believe it or not, all of this helped me become a better writer because it improved my communication skills, allowed me to connect with others and gave me the confidence I needed to stop hiding from the world.

I don't want you to misunderstand, I am still a huge introvert who loves sitting at home by myself and writing books. But I know deep down that was not the sole (soul) purpose of my life. My inner voice told me I had to get out into the world and connect with others through networking, speaking and teaching.

As a result of listening to my inner voice, I now have a very successful business where I get to do things I love like writing books, teaching, hosting writer's retreats like www.ocean-writing.com, and helping clients with their books.

Public speaking made me a better writer and gave me more things to write about.

Listen to your inner voice, even if it makes no logical sense. Pay close attention; especially if it is relentless and keeps saying the same thing.

Notes

_____

_____

_____

_____

_____

_____

_____

_____

_____

_____

_____

_____

_____

_____

_____

_____

_____

_____

Chapter 23: Suffering

What has your suffering taught you?

"Some people once brought a blind man to Jesus and asked him, 'Rabbi, who sinned, this man or his parents, that he was born blind?' They all wanted to know why this terrible curse had fallen on this man.
And Jesus answered, 'It was not that this man sinned or his parents, but that the words of God might be manifest in him'. He told them not to look for why the suffering came, but to listen for what the suffering could teach them."

–Wayne Miller

Suffering is our greatest teacher and is also a necessary step to evolving and transforming our lives. Of course, we have the choice to be a victim of our suffering or to learn from our suffering.

My suffering has taught me to pay attention to my inner voice, my heart and my soul. It reminds me that when I don't listen to that still voice within, then my life gets painful and difficult.

We can't escape suffering. No one is exempt from it. We can have a pity party for ourselves, but if we stay in that state of mind we become victims.

David R. Hawkins, M.D., Ph.D., in his bestselling book, *Power vs. Force: The Hidden Determinants of Human Behavior* says, "It isn't life's events, but how one reacts to them and the attitude that one has about that, that determines whether such events have a positive or negative effect on one's life, whether they're experienced as *opportunity* or as *stress*."

He goes on to say that nothing has the power to create stress. A divorce may be traumatic if it's unwanted or a release into freedom if it's desired.

When we feel powerless, we feel like we are at the mercy of life and that the source of our happiness, or unhappiness, is "out there."

When we take back our power, we realize the source of our happiness is within ourselves.

Victor Frankl, Austrian psychiatrist and Holocaust survivor is well known for his book, *Man's Search for Meaning* — a meditation on what the gruesome experience of Auschwitz taught him about the primary purpose of life: the quest for meaning, which sustained those who survived.

For Frankl, meaning came from three possible sources: purposeful work, love, and courage in the face of difficulty.

Frankl reminds us, "Everything can be taken from a man but one thing: the last of the human freedoms — to choose one's attitude in any given set of circumstances, to choose one's own way."

Learn from your suffering and choose not to be a victim.

What has your suffering taught you?

Notes

Bonus Question: Waiting

In what ways are you "waiting" to start living?

Eckhart Tolle, a prolific spiritual author of transformational books like *A New Earth* and *The Power of Now*, says:

"Large scale waiting is waiting for the next vacation, for a better job, for the children to grow up, for a truly meaningful relationship, for success, to make money, to be important, to become enlightened. It is not uncommon for people to spend their whole life *waiting* to start living."

Seems sad, but it's true. We all have played the waiting game. Waiting for a promotion, waiting for our perfect house, perfect job, or perfect relationship in order to be "happy".

When we choose external things in order to be happy, then what happens if those things don't come to fruition?

It means we are wasting precious time, not allowing ourselves to be happy in the present.

It doesn't mean that we can't *desire* a better job, relationship, house or situation, it's just that if we are waiting for that event to happen in order to be happy, then the waiting time is time wasted by not living in the present moment.

What activities or non-activities bring you back to the present moment?

For me, it's being out in nature and near the water. Also feeling sick or having an injury brings me to the present because it makes everything else seem less important. Meditation helps me be more present. When we are truly present, we aren't worrying about the future or spending time regretting the past.

The World Health Organization has named depression as the greatest cause of suffering worldwide. In the U.S., 1 out of 5 people deal with depression or anxiety. For youth, that number increases to 1 in 3.

The good news is that 40% of our happiness can be influenced by intentional thoughts and actions, leading to life changing habits.

We do choose our thoughts, however, we don't have to be a victim of them. When we are not living in the present moment, we can easily become a victim of our negative thoughts.

In the #1 New York Times bestselling book by Michael Singer, *The Untethered Soul*, he says that we have two voices inside of us – one is our habitual voice (narrating voice) or what he refers to as our inner roommate and the other is the observer.

He goes on to say:

"Problems are generally not what they appear to be. When you get clear enough, you will realize that the real problem is that there is something inside of you that can have a problem with almost anything. The first step is to deal with that part of you... You have to break the habit of thinking that the solution to your problems is to rearrange things outside. The only permanent solution to your problems is to go inside and let go of the part of you that seems to have so many problems with reality."

Here is an excerpt from Oprah.com about author Bryon Katie and her view on suffering:

"All the suffering that goes on inside our minds is not reality, says Byron Katie, it's just a story we torture ourselves with." She has a simple, completely replicable system for freeing ourselves of the thoughts that make us suffer. "All war begins on paper," she explains. You write down your stressful thoughts, and then ask yourself the following four questions:

Question 1: Is it true?

This question can change your life. Be still and ask yourself if the thought you wrote down is true.

Question 2: Can you absolutely know it's true?

This is another opportunity to open your mind and to go deeper into the unknown to find the answers that live beneath what we think we know.

Question 3: How do you react—what happens—when you believe that thought?

With this question, you begin to notice internal cause and effect. You can see that when you believe the thought, there is a disturbance that can range from mild discomfort to fear or panic. What do you feel? How do you treat the person (or the situation) you've written about, how do you treat yourself, when you believe that thought? Make a list, and be specific.

Question 4: Who would you be without the thought?

Imagine yourself in the presence of that person (or in that situation), without believing the thought. How would your life be different if you didn't have the ability to even think the stressful thought? How would you feel? Which do you pre-fer—life with or without the thought? Which feels kinder, more peaceful?

Turn the thought around:

The "turnaround" gives you an opportunity to experience the opposite of what you believe. Once you have found one or more turnarounds to your original statement, you are in-vited to find at least three specific, genuine examples of how each turnaround is true in your life.

****

We need to stop waiting for some future event to happen before we can be happy. Happiness is a choice.

It's important to observe what you are "waiting for" so that you don't let life pass you by.

List three things you are waiting for right now to be happy.

Years ago, I hired a career coach because I was so miserable in my legal job. While I was building my online business part time on the side, she encouraged me to transform my thoughts about my law firm job and to start seeing it as a means to an end. My legal job paid the bills, took care of my family and allowed me to build my online business part time. It also gave me many of the skills I needed to build my online business.

So instead of thinking I couldn't be happy until I was free from my legal job, I turned my thinking around to enjoying the present moment more and knowing that while I was working toward something greater, I could be happy with where I was too.

Where are you playing the waiting game in your life? How can you appreciate what you have now and be happy in this moment.

Like Mel Robbins, Life Coach and author of the bestselling book, *The 5 Second Rule* says, "If a problem can be solved by action, then you really don't have a problem."

So, if you're in a bad relationship that is sucking the energy out of you, you can leave that relationship. Same with a bad job or a stressful situation.

If you can't leave it, then you can transform your thoughts about the current situation so you are at peace about it.

Notes

Closing Thoughts

Finding your passion isn't a one and done event.

I think our passions change and constantly evolve during our lives, and if we pay attention to our heart and soul, we can live our passions every day.

We don't have to think "large scale" or "change the world" passions, but we do need to think about the simple everyday things that make us happy and bring us joy.

A few additional questions to ponder:

- What gives you energy and what depletes your energy?

- What do you want more of in your life and less of in your life?

For anything you want in your life, answer the question:

In order to have _____, this must die _____.

In nature, there is a natural life-death-life cycle.

In her book, *Women Who Run With the Wolves*, author Clarissa Pinkola Estes, says:

"The only trust required is to know that when there is one ending there will be another beginning."

We are always creating. We are born to create.

Live your life more by your curiosities than by your fears and you will find yourself happier, more joyful and more energetic.

Go forth and create a passion-filled life.

The treasures are hidden inside of you waiting for you to say "Yes"!

Notes

_____

_____

_____

_____

_____

_____

_____

_____

_____

_____

_____

_____

_____

_____

_____

_____

About Michelle Kulp

Michelle Kulp, is passionate about teaching women to find their purpose, passion and calling and creating their Dream Life!

Website/Blog: **www.becomea6figurewoman.com**

Motto: "Build a Life that Nourishes Your Soul!"

Advice: "Do What You Love! Love What You Do!"

*   *   *   *   *   *   *   *

In 2000, after a 17 year career in the legal field, Michelle was "let go" from her job at the law firm. At the time she was feeling extremely unfulfilled, drained and confused. After she left her legal job, she decided to follow her passions and her intuition and stop making the "safe" choices. She pursued her writing passion and became a reporter for a few years. She also pursued her love of teaching and writing and started her online business in 2005:

www.becomea6figurewoman.com

Michelle helps women transform their intellectual knowledge into PLAY-CHECKS, not PAY-CHECKS!

> *"Freedom is what motivates me as I was trapped in a cubicle for 17 years and I'm never going back to that corporate prison!"*

Michelle also helps her clients write, publish and profit from bestselling books through her *"Bestselling Author Program"*. Getting a book published and on the Bestsellers list, not only helps with lead generation, but also helps boost her client's credibility so they are seen as the "go-to" expert in their field. And of course, the added benefit of creating another stream of online income!

Michelle teaches, *"Do the work once and get paid over and over so you can leverage your time.* When you have multiple streams of income and you are selling your knowledge and expertise, then you will have more freedom in your life.

Many of Michelle's clients are #1 bestselling authors and have gone on to create successful coaching, consulting, speaking and online businesses.

Michelle is the bestselling author of several books on Amazon including: **Quit Your Job and Follow your Dreams: A 12 Month Guide to Becoming Joyfully Jobless; I Love Myself When; Woman Take Hold of Your Power, Ocean Writing, Never Work Again: 6 Secrets to Earning a Play-Check Instead of a Pay-Check, and Backwards Book Launch.**

.

Made in the USA
Monee, IL
16 December 2020